Soul of Brussels

A GUIDE TO EXCEPTIONAL EXPERIENCES

WRITTEN BY ISABELLE DOUILLET-DE PANGE
ILLUSTRATED BY ALLILALU

JONGLEZ PUBLISHING

Travel guides

OOPS!

Perfectly imperfect.

(BRUSSELS SLOGAN)

While Europe's great capitals dazzle with their elegance, spotless pavements and carefully restored monuments, Brussels presents a rather different picture – with its relentless rain, perplexing politics, 183 nationalities, somewhat uninspiring canal, peeing child statue (known as the Manneken Pis) and oversized balls ...

And yet, believe it or not, we love it – and you will too.

Here, there's no need to live up to anything except yourself. Everyone does, in their own way – with their virtues, flaws, language, heritage (whether rich or poor) and their dreams. There's beauty here, but you have to track it down. And then there's that unmistakable whiff of surrealism in the air – a feeling that nothing here is ever too serious, just endlessly amusing.

In this guide, we'll take you here, there and everywhere – from the heart of the city to some of its lesser-known outskirts. We've untangled the threads of this curious capital to create a seamless itinerary for you – one that invites you to explore, laugh and ease yourself into the rhythm of this quirky place.

We've asked our friends to help uncover the best tips and hidden gems. If you're an Instagrammer, capturing the perfect shot might prove challenging. But if you like to live life to the full, you'll be in heaven here. This city is a true living ecosystem – abundant, vibrant and teeming with diversity. For some mysterious reason, the world gathers here. Is it for the fries, the chocolates, the beer or the peculiar charm of our French accent? We couldn't say, and honestly, we don't care. What matters is that everyone is here, together – and that's what makes it special.

So join the dance, wander the glistening cobblestones, steal kisses in bars, shoo away the pigeons and enjoy! Embrace the city and its spirit ... and let it carry you wherever it may lead.

SO, SHALL WE GO LEFT OR RIGHT?
LET'S GO LEFT AND RIGHT.

WHAT YOU WON'T FIND IN THIS GUIDE

- A map of the metro (it's confusing, anyway)
- The most boring Michelin-starred restaurants
- The exact height of the Manneken Pis
- Practical details about the Atomium

WHAT YOU WILL FIND IN THIS GUIDE

- A once-fabled lover's inn that's now a hotel
- Little-known art nouveau gems
- How to reach for the clouds
- The best indulgences, from fries to pralines
- A sanctuary hidden in a forest
- The secrets of the Court House

Most of all, you'll get closer to the soul of Brussels – a chaotic, surprising and deeply endearing city. And the promise of an unforgettable journey.

KEY TO THE SYMBOLS USED IN **SOUL OF BRUSSELS**

Budget-friendly

Mid-range

Expensive

Best in summer

Reservations recommended

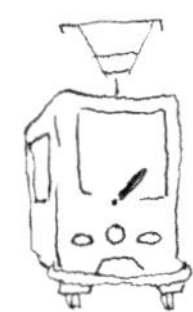

Accessible by public transport

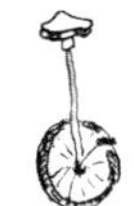

Walkable from the city centre

Opening times often vary,
so we recommend checking them directly
on the website of the place you plan to visit.

30 EXPERIENCES

01. A chocolatier with flair
02. Experience ... the Marolles
03. The double life of Brigitte
04. Staying hydrated in the clouds
05. Sleeping (and dreaming) in the world's most beautiful square
06. The fakir's predictions
07. The many cuisines of Brussels
08. The night becomes you
09. Fresh fish, get your fresh fish!
10. Enjoy a beer in a hospice
11. Swinging in a church
12. It's a whale!
13. The magic of film (history)
14. Discovering the city's bowels
15. Brussels loves beer!
16. The secret temple of the night
17. In fries we trust
18. Art nouveau, Blérot and a good sleep
19. The elusive abbey
20. The poisonous beauty of art nouveau
21. Not all art is cast away
22. Hallucinate in a historic house
23. An urban planning mistake that only Brussels can claim
24. Closer to heaven
25. The most beautiful greenhouses in the world
26. Already a taste of the forest
27. A cathedral of trees
28. The *enfant terrible* of Brussel's gastronomy
29. Listen to the beating heart of old Anderlecht
30. And what if the masterpiece was the city itself?

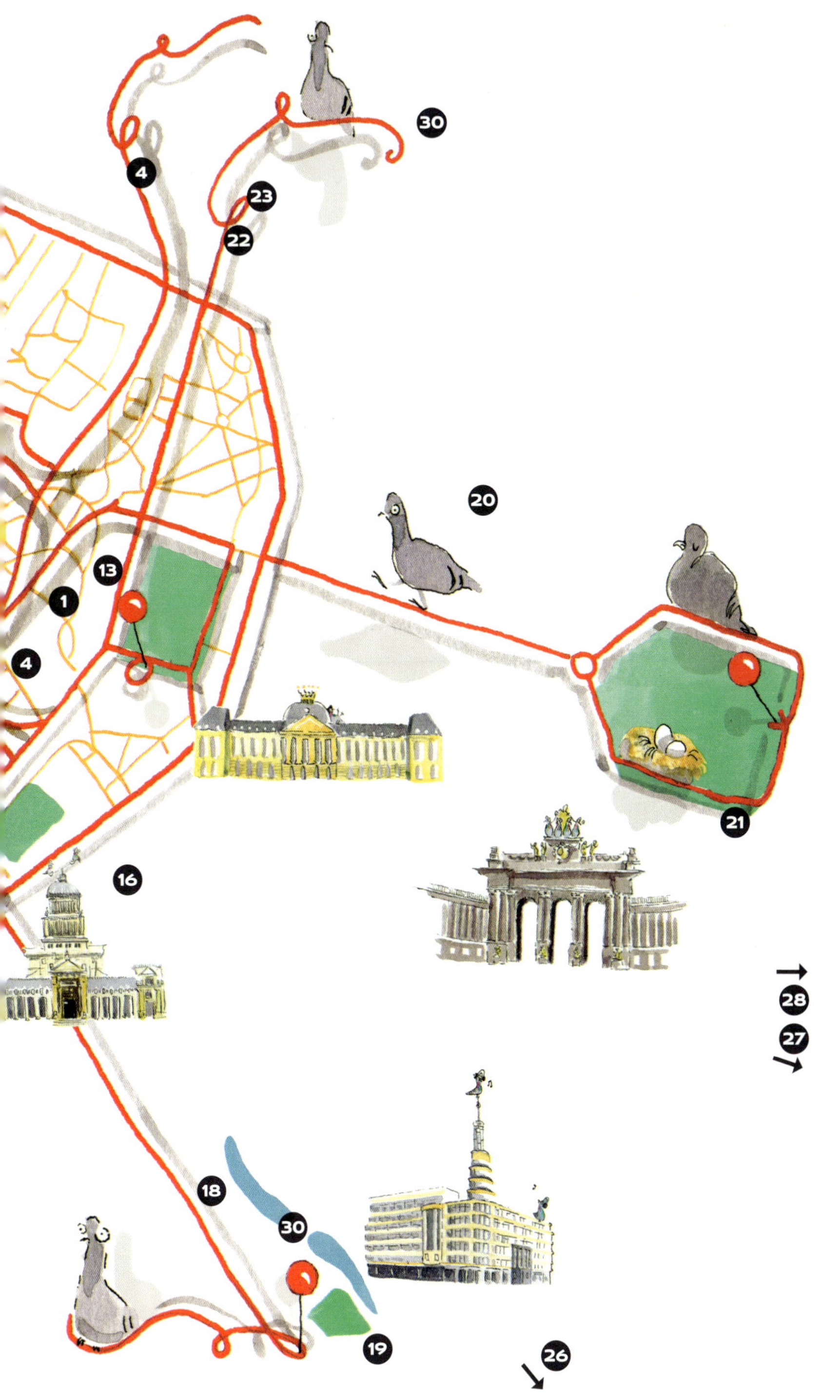
30
4
23
22
20
13
1
4
21
16
28
27
18
30
19
26

A CHOCOLATIER WITH FLAIR

Laurent Gerbaud is the darling of the Brussels chocolate scene, bringing fresh energy to the city's love for pralines – those delicious filled chocolates that Belgians adore.

The multi-award-winning chocolatier wins hearts not only with his exquisite creations but also with his warm and charismatic personality. Passionate, jovial and approachable, he personally leads a workshop every Saturday, where participants learn to craft *mendiants* (a traditional confection composed of a chocolate disk studded with nuts and dried fruits) and, more importantly, to savour the rich tapestry of flavours that chocolate offers. From Madagascar to Venezuela and Nicaragua, this sensory journey is as delightful as it is transformative. Few things are as entertaining – or satisfying – as refining your palate.

LAURENT GERBAUD CHOCOLATIER
2D, RUE RAVENSTEIN
1000 BRUXELLES

chocolatsgerbaud.be
Instagram: @laurentgerbaud

Metro stop: Parc or Gare Centrale

© LAURENT GERBAUD

Located opposite Bozar (Centre for Fine Arts), the shop is a cheerful hive of activity. Pralines are crafted right before your eyes, celebrities and politicians drop in, and regulars enjoy steaming mugs of hot chocolate. Treat yourself to the joy of chocolate-dipped fruits, ganaches bursting with flavour and other irresistibly unique creations that are as surprising as they are addictive.

EXPERIENCE ...
THE MAROLLES

The Marolles district is, in itself, a fabulous experience. At its heart lies the Place du Jeu de Balle, where every morning – yes, every morning! – the flea market takes place. For just a few euros, you can find the most unexpected items, from vintage furniture to all sorts of clothing. You haggle, laugh, search and marvel. It's a daily treasure hunt, enjoyable not only for the great bargains but also for the friendly atmosphere.

The flea market extends its charm throughout the neighbourhood, with cafés and restaurants to take a break from shopping, as well as antique shops, decor stores and thrift shops to continue the hunt.

Interestingly, the spirit of Brussels thrives in this vibrant area. It was here that the painter Bruegel lived in the 16th century (be sure to visit his tomb in the Chapelle Church) and it was from this very place that riots broke out against the Court House during its inauguration in 1886.

MARCHÉ AUX PUCES (FLEA MARKET)
PLACE DU JEU DE BALLE
1000 BRUXELLES

MON-FRI: 9am / 2pm
SAT & SUN: 9am / 3pm

Metro stop: Porte Louise

BAINS
BADEN

© ARTÈR

> One of the unusual hidden spots in the Marolles is the Piscine du Centre, built in the early 1950s on the site of an old dead-end street. Architect Maurice Van Nieuwenhuyse had to work with a particularly narrow plot, leading him to stack the two pools on top of each other. Thus, the large swimming pool is located on the third floor ... What could be more delightful than taking a short swim while enjoying the city skyline? Visit in the late afternoon for total peace.

PISCINE DU CENTRE
28, RUE DU CHEVREUIL
1000 BRUXELLES

bainbadbxl.be/web/be/page/piscine-du-centre

© VICTOR PATYN

> Versus is simply beautiful. Set in an old hat shop from 1900, it offers an alternative and appealing vision of a florist, where eco-circularity and respect for the environment are taken seriously. Daphné, the aptly named owner, organises workshops and classes – a chance to connect with flowers with the help of an enchantress who knows their language.

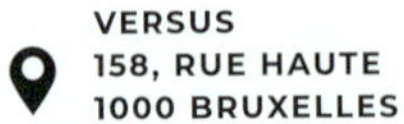

VERSUS
158, RUE HAUTE
1000 BRUXELLES

versusfleurs.be

Instagram: @versus_bxl

> Here, time stands still, but life still pulses. Mademoiselle l'Ancien is a world filled with memories carried by clothes from the past. Two women preside over these treasures, and with their discerning gaze, they breathe new life into them by sharing their stories and adapting them to your body. With intricate cuts, refined details and rare pieces, it's a unique thrift shopping experience.

MADEMOISELLE L'ANCIEN
127, RUE HAUTE
1000 BRUXELLES

mademoisellelancien.be

Instagram: @mademoisellelancien

© ROMAIN VENNEKENS

THE DOUBLE LIFE OF BRIGITTE

On the edge of the Marolles district are two Brussels institutions that, strangely enough, share the same name: the Brigittines. One is a temple of dance, the other a haven for local gastronomy. This name harks back to the former convent that stood here until the late 18th century, of which only a small church remains (see 'Brigitte dances', following double page).

These two venues are set against a typical backdrop that illustrates how deeply rooted urban planning is in Brussels. In the heart of the city, six elevated railway lines cut across the area. In the first half of the 20th century, there was a scheme to connect all the main train stations in the capital, and ... it was done! This disruption of the old neighbourhoods would be almost amusing if it weren't for the surrounding homes.

However, you already know enough about Brussels to understand that it is in such seemingly unfortunate places that magic happens. So do step inside these Brigittines.

© LES BRIGITTINES

> **Brigitte dances:**

Brussels boasts a vibrant contemporary dance scene full of experimentation, collaboration and distinctive personalities. Les Brigittines stands out as one of the key venues. Each season brings new creations, residencies and workshops. It's exciting, liberating and often exceptional. Inside the old baroque church, modern performances are enhanced by the building's timeworn features. Outside, you'll notice that the church has received a contemporary 'twin', a stunning extension made of glass and Corten steel designed by architect Andrea Bruno.

LES BRIGITTINES
PETITE RUE DES BRIGITTINES
1000 BRUXELLES

brigittines.be

Instagram: @lesbrigittines

© ANNE CLAPDORP

> **Brigitte dines:**

From the moment you step inside, you're met with a warm and friendly atmosphere: an old counter, Thonet chairs, soft lighting, green walls, a large fireplace and lovely staff – just the right balance. Dirk Myny, the heart and soul of the place, is there to greet you. He's a true Brussels local and we love him for it. The cuisine draws inspiration from the brasserie style: nothing new, yet it feels as if you're tasting it for the very first time. Everything is revitalised, fresh, delicious and generous. Yum!

LES BRIGITTINES
5, PLACE DE LA CHAPELLE
1000 BRUXELLES

+32 2 512 68 91
lesbrigittines.com

Instagram: @restaurant.les.brigittines

STAYING HYDRATED **IN THE CLOUDS**

'With a sky so grey that a canal has hung itself,' sang Jacques Brel. Full of despair, the somewhat melancholic Belgian singer neglected to mention that when the sky isn't grey and low – which does happen sometimes – it is absolutely wonderful. Inspired by Magritte, the clouds are part of Brussels' scenery. When evening falls, it's not uncommon to see the the sky light up in orange, pink and violet. Simply stunning.

It's no wonder rooftops abound. Over the past few years, they've sprouted up like mushrooms, offering new perspectives and a chance to rise above the city. Here's a tour of our favourites:

©JULIEN DEWARICHET

> **Albert:** Located on the 5th floor of the esteemed Royal Library of Belgium (KBR), this panoramic restaurant offers delicious, fresh cuisine (the shrimp croquettes are divine). The cherry on the top? Its 1950s' furniture, from the old staff cafeteria, perfectly captures the nostalgic Belgian 'modernity' of yesteryear!

ALBERT
28, MONT DES ARTS
1000 BRUXELLES

+32 465 04 83 31
Instagram: @albertbrussels

Main entrance to KBR, go up to the 5th floor

BEERLAB

©JULIEN DEWARICHET

> **Beerlab:** The brand-new Beerlab sits atop the old stock exchange, now transformed into a centre dedicated to beer. The terrace is vast and still relatively unknown, with a particularly lovely view of the lower city. The drinks menu lives up to expectations, featuring 150 types of beer, including 49 on tap.

> **Tope:** Near the North Station, perched atop a former office tower repurposed as a hotel (The Hoxton), is this surprising rooftop serving Mexican flavours. The cocktails pack a punch!

BEERLAB
80, BOULEVARD ANSPACH
1000 BRUXELLES

belgianbeerworld.be
Instagram: @thebeerlab.brussels

TOPE
1, SQUARE VICTORIA RÉGINA
1210 SAINT-JOSSE-TEN-NOODE

thehoxton.com
Instagram: @tope_brussels

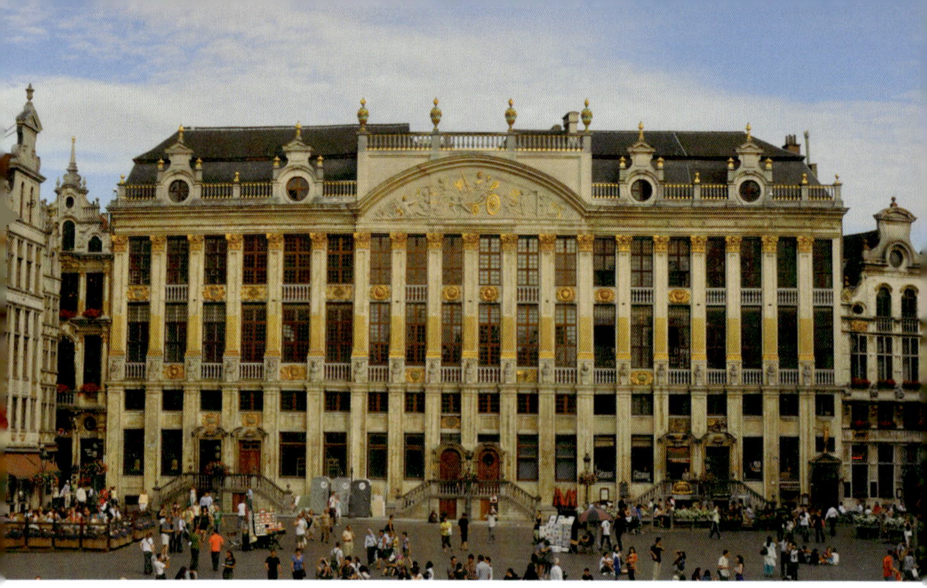

LE QUINZE
RESIDENCE HOTEL
15
RESTAURANT
'T KELDERKE

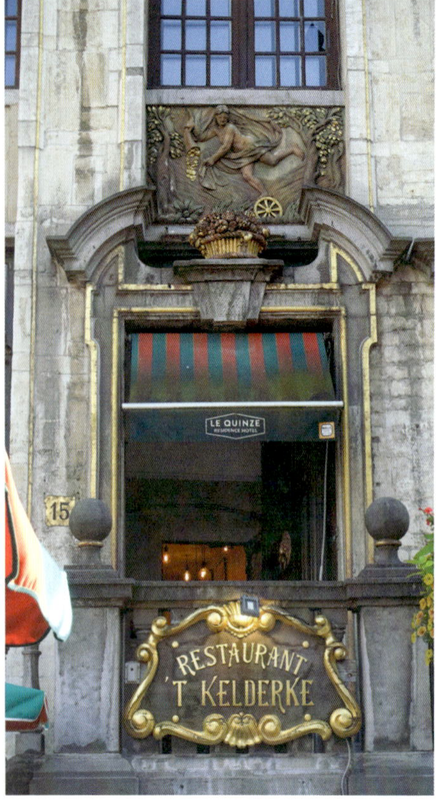

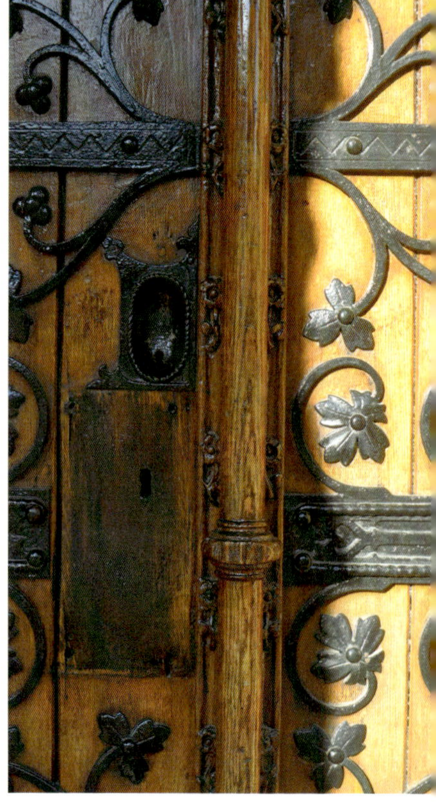

SLEEPING (AND DREAMING) **IN THE WORLD'S MOST BEAUTIFUL SQUARE**

For the people of Brussels, this is the most beautiful square in the world – and honestly, it really is! Dominated by its grand 15th-century town hall, the 16th-century King's House and the guild houses from the late 17th century, the Grand-Place effortlessly combines various architectural styles, showcasing its vibrant beauty with golden details and statues perched atop gables.

Surprisingly, there is only one hotel located in the buildings, allowing guests to spend the night with wide-open windows overlooking this stunning backdrop. Simple yet offering excellent value for money, Le Quinze features seven rooms with views of the square (make sure to request one of these). After soaking in the breathtaking sights, you'll be invited to enjoy breakfast on the opposite side of the square at a charming establishment called La Brouette (all the buildings have names). All in all, an unforgettable experience!

LE QUINZE HOTEL
15, GRAND-PLACE
1000 BRUXELLES

+32 2 511 09 56 | hotel-le-quinze-grand-place.be | Metro and bus stops: Gare Centrale

Do you love the city centre? So do we.

Just a stone's throw from the Monnaie Opera is a historic building dating from 1888. The former General Savings and Pensions Bank, designed by renowned 19th-century Belgian architect Henri Beyaert, has recently been converted into the elegantly named Fleur de Ville hotel.

Expect chic, plush rooms and a beautifully preserved historic decor.

FLEUR DE VILLE HOTEL
46B, RUE DU FOSSÉ AUX LOUPS
1000 BRUXELLES

+ 32 2 206 10 30
hotelfleurdeville.com

Metro stop: De Brouckère

THE FAKIR'S PREDICTIONS

Nestled in one of the small brick houses in the city centre, opposite the baroque facade of the Riches-Claires Church, Booze 'n' Blues exudes a slightly seedy charm that's hard to resist. It's the perfect spot to enjoy local beers and live music, but most of all, to reconnect with a sense of authenticity in a world polished to the bone.

But there's another reason to go: the fakir. The fakir? Yes, *the* fakir. Sitting proudly on the counter is a century-old varnished pine box featuring a fakir with a needle. For the modest sum of 20 cents, the fakir will point the needle towards a prophecy or a piece of advice. From 'Avoid distant travels' to 'One true love will fill your heart' or the classic 'Good fortune and a hefty inheritance are on the way,' you'll leave forewarned. And as they say, to be forewarned is to be forearmed ...

BOOZE 'N' BLUES BAR
20, RUE DES RICHES-CLAIRES
1000 BRUXELLES

Instagram: @Booze 'n' Blues

Metro stop: Bourse or De Brouckère

DULLE WIND 4.5€
TEXACO ETHYL
20 CENT
SUCCESS IN LOVE AND WEALTH
SOMEONE LOVES YOU MADLY
GOOD NEWS IS ON THE WAY
HAPPINESS LIES AT HOME
A DARK-HAIRED LADY TAKES AN INTEREST IN YOU
BEWARE OF THAT DODGY PERSON
YOU'RE LUCKIER THAN YOU DESERVE
YOU'LL SOON BE TALKING TO A BUSINESSMAN
AVOID DISTANT TRAVELS
OFF WE GO!
YOU WILL BE POWERLESS BEFORE THEIR LOVE

PHOTOS © JULIEN DEWARICHET

MANNEKEN PIS CAFÉ

THE MANY CUISINES OF BRUSSELS

The diverse cuisines of Brussels capture the essence of all the regions of the small country of Belgium. Shrimp croquettes, mussels and cod bring you to the beaches of the North Sea, while Flemish beef stew takes you back to the countryside, and Liège salad leads you to the Meuse region. Endives *au gratin* are a Brussels speciality, with chicory traditionally grown around the capital. Don't miss the classic *waterzooi* (a type of stew made with fish or chicken) or *stoemp* (a chunky mash of potatoes and seasonal vegetables served with a hearty country sausage).

> **In't Spinnekopke:** One of the oldest restaurants in the city, located in a quiet square on the edge of the city centre. With its original woodwork, old furnishings and low beams, this tavern takes you back in time. The cuisine is typical of Brussels, using local and seasonal ingredients.

IN'T SPINNEKOPKE
1, PLACE DU JARDIN AUX FLEURS
1000 BRUXELLES

+32 2 305 56 65

spinnekopje.be

> **Manneken-Pis Café:** One of the best spots in the city centre, right across from the little pissing boy on the first floor. It has a warm atmosphere and serves a modern take on Belgian cuisine.

Absolutely top-notch!

MANNEKEN PIS CAFÉ
31, RUE DES GRANDS CARMES
1000 BRUXELLES

mannekenpiscafe.com

Instagram: @mannekenpis.cafe

THE NIGHT
BECOMES YOU

L'Archiduc is one of the most iconic spots in the capital, offering a deep dive into jazz, modernist influences and the powerful charm of the 1930s.

Since 1937, it has been a haven for musicians, from the Belgian singer Arno to Lady Gaga, night owls, cocktail enthusiasts and whisky lovers – a place for intimate conversations on velvet sofas. On Saturdays and Sundays, enjoy jazz concerts in the late afternoon. Otherwise, you can drop by every day until 5am ...

L'ARCHIDUC
6, RUE ANTOINE DANSAERT
1000 BRUXELLES

archiduc.com

Instagram: @larchiduc

© L'ARCHIDUC

NoordZEE
Mer du Nord
GUDULE!
YOUR KIBBELIN
ARE READY!

FRESH FISH, **GET YOUR FRESH FISH!**

We are here in the heart of the lower town, on Rue Sainte-Catherine, one of the oldest streets in Brussels. With its cobblestones and traditional gabled houses with stepped or scroll roofs, it feels like stepping into a postcard ... if it weren't for the lively and somewhat chaotic atmosphere.

At the corner of Place Sainte-Catherine stands a Brussels institution: De Noordzee. On sunny days, this excellent fish shop has high tables set up in the square. You order at the counter and when your dish is ready, the waitress shouts your name into the crowd to find you on the terrace. Simple, efficient and friendly.

On the menu are grilled fish, fried fish and fish soup: everything is fresh, quick and tasty at this delightful fish bar.

DE NOORDZEE FISH SHOP
45, RUE SAINTE-CATHERINE
1000 BRUXELLES

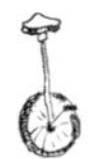

Metro stop: Sainte-Catherine

ENJOY A BEER **IN A HOSPICE**

While the city centre bustles with activity, there lies a peaceful, white-hued district – the former *béguinage*, a historical complex where lay nuns lived in a community without taking formal vows – dominated by its beautiful baroque church dedicated to St John the Baptist. In this lesser-known part of the city centre stands the Grand Hospice. This early 19th-century building, with its understated neoclassical design, once served as a refuge for the elderly and infirm, with strict divisions between men and women around two central courtyards.

LE GRAND HOSPICE
7, RUE DU GRAND HOSPICE
1000 BRUXELLES

From May to September	grand-hospice.brussels Instagram: @grand.hospice	Metro stop: Sainte-Catherine

Times have changed. Long abandoned and awaiting renovation, this vast hospice now hosts a variety of artistic, ecological and community initiatives. The result is an extraordinary ecosystem that greets visitors as soon as they enter. Old trees, outdoor cafés, *pétanque* courts, yoga sessions and much more create a welcoming atmosphere – perfect for relaxing on a warm afternoon or evening.

© GORDON DELACROIX

Jardin

SWINGING IN A CHURCH

Welcome to pure eccentricity: we ask for your discretion and respect for this unusual and slightly surreal initiative. It takes place in the lovely baroque church of Notre-Dame de Bon Secours, directly opposite a bar called Au Soleil that's popular with locals.

Inside this 17th-century church, two swings have been hung from the organ's choir loft. They allow visitors to sway peacefully, creating a delightful, hypnotic sensation. The hexagonal layout of the building, its dome adorned with chubby little cherubs, oak confessionals and white stone pillars – all of this baroque scenery gently passes before you as you swing back and forth. Guaranteed pleasure and serenity await. But shh! Promise?

NOTRE-DAME DE BON SECOURS
91, RUE DU MARCHÉ AU CHARBON
1000 BRUXELLES

Free entry	Metro stop: Gare Centrale

IT'S **A WHALE!**

Strangely enough, Brussels has some gigantic monuments and no one cares. One of them is the Court House. Built between 1866 and 1886, this behemoth is so titanically proportioned that it makes you dizzy. Built on a 150 x 160 metre quadrilateral, it covers 26,000 square metres of floor space, under a 105-metre-high dome. In the 19th century, it was quite simply the largest monument in the world!

The people of Brussels don't like anything that sticks out. As a result, the building is generally shunned. Yet immersing yourself in it is an experience in itself. Once past the scaffolding on the facades (still under construction!), you enter some fascinating spaces, where references to Babylon, ancient Egypt and ancient Rome are legion. The interiors are mind-blowing and you won't want to miss the fabulous 300-step interior staircase leading down to the Marolles.

PALAIS DE JUSTICE (COURTHOUSE)
PLACE POELAERT
1000 BRUXELLES

arkadia.be (French) or korei.be (English)

© OPHELIA CHERRY - PIXABAY

© BOYS IN BRISTOL PHOTOGRAPHY - PEXELS

© LAURENT VERDIER - PIXABAY

1
7
8
2
3
9
10
5
15
16
11
17
12
18
24
25

THE MAGIC OF **FILM (HISTORY)**

Housed in the Palais des Beaux-Arts (Bozar), which dates back to the art deco period and was designed by the famous architect Victor Horta, the Royal Belgian Film Archive has one of the finest film collections in the world, which it conserves and restores while opening it to the public.

Two screening rooms offer an exciting programme of films every day, at reasonable prices. Most of them come from film stock preserved by the institution. The result is a vintage feel, an unexpected delight for eyes used to digital films.

What's more – and this is one of the Cinematek's musts – the silent films are accompanied by a live pianist who improvises along with the images.

CINEMATEK
9, RUE BARON HORTA
1000 BRUXELLES

cinematek.be
Instagram: @cinematekbe

Metro stop: Gare Centrale or Parc

© CAMILLE VAN DURME

As soon as you enter, you are plunged into the magic of cinema. A cabinet of curiosities displays a whole series of pre-cinema objects with strange names and amusing functions: Kinetoscope, Praxinoscope, Phenakistoscope and other Thaumatropes. Film lovers rejoice!

GRAND ELDORADO

Like all major European cities, Brussels boasts more than one exceptional cinema.

Among them, we have a soft spot for:

> **Grand Eldorado:**

Within the UGC De Brouckère complex, one cinema is particularly worth a visit – the former Grand Eldorado. Stepping inside is like diving into Belgium's colonial past, with its gilded fresco depicting elephants, jungle landscapes and banana trees.

38, place de Brouckère - 1000 Bruxelles

ugc.be

> **Nova:**

No art deco grandeur or mainstream blockbusters here, just a boldly alternative approach. Nova shines a spotlight on independent fiction, short films and thought-provoking documentaries, often rare and socially engaged. It's raw, it's powerful and it shakes things up. And frankly, we could all use a bit of that.

3, rue d'Arenberg – 1000 Bruxelles

nova-cinema.org

DISCOVERING **THE CITY'S BOWELS**

The Brussels Sewer Museum is one of the most fascinating of its kind. Firstly, because of the way it's set up: you enter through a former toll house and leave through the identical one opposite. Between the two, the route takes you to the small river that once flowed through the centre and gave birth to the city. This is the Senne, a capricious and meandering river, a far cry from its majestic Parisian counterpart, the Seine. Vaults were built over the Senne at the end of the 19th century in an attempt to stop it flooding. The tour takes you through one of the openings where it is now enclosed.

But that's not all. Once you've passed the Senne, you'll find yourself walking through a large sewer, where wastewater flows downhill. It's easy to see that each street has its own underground sewer that runs beneath it.

MUSÉE DES ÉGOUTS
PORTE D'ANDERLECHT
1000 BRUXELLES

Heavy rain may disrupt the visit, check on:
sewermuseum.brussels
Instagram: @sewermuseum

Tram stop: Porte d'Anderlecht

© MILESTONE PRODUCITONS

Even allowing for a certain squeamishness on the part of some visitors, the fact remains that being able to descend into the bowels of the city in this way is not only a fascinating experience for understanding its ecosystem, but also an extraordinarily rare one.

SEWER RAT

BRUSSELS **LOVES BEER!**

Beer and Brussels have been intertwined for centuries. Even today, microbreweries are popping up all over the city, constantly updating this age-old craft.

To explore this, there's no better place than the Cantillon Brewery, the last of its kind still brewing lambic, a spontaneously fermented beer. This family-run brewery takes you back in time; nothing has changed since it was established in 1900. Even now, it continues to produce and export its products worldwide while showcasing its work – a true living museum.

Instead of wandering around alone, it's best to join a guided tour. These take place on Saturdays and are followed by a tasting.

BRASSERIE CANTILLON/
MUSÉE BRUXELLOIS DE LA GUEUZE
56, RUE GHEUDE
1070 BRUXELLES

cantillon.be

Bus, metro and tram stops: Gare du Midi

THE SECRET TEMPLE OF THE NIGHT

Few hotels have the power to transport us to another dimension, but Le Berger hotel, just a few steps from Avenue Louise, is one of them.

This hotel openly embraces its former life as a clandestine meeting place, a discreet haven where fleeting lovers and forbidden romances once converged. There's nothing sordid about it, though – only an air of mystery heightened by its art deco charm: the sleek curves of the furniture, the intricate wallpaper and the rich wood panelling. The narrow, winding hallways seem to invite stolen kisses.

LE BERGER HOTEL
24, RUE DU BERGER
1050 BRUXELLES

+32 472 01 75 11

leberger hotel.be
Instagram: @le.berger.hotel

Metro stop: Porte de Namur

The history of Le Berger is as improbable as it is fascinating. Built in 1935 and miraculously preserved, it faced demolition in 2010. Enter Isabelle Léonard, whose unwavering determination saved the building – and its soul – from the real-estate developers.

She succeeded, and today its 51 rooms, each named after a woman (Jeanne, Antoinette, Ambre ...), offer unique worlds of sensuality and intrigue, inviting guests to indulge in the art of seduction.

The design leaves little to the imagination: freestanding bathtubs and showers are often placed with daring intentionality, unashamedly close to the bed.

Opt for one of the original rooms from Le Berger's early days, whether standard or superior, and enjoy the experience.

Live it fully, with your beloved.

"T'AS PAS TOUTES
LES GAUFRITES DANS
LE MÊME SACHET."
FERNAND OBB

IN FRIES
WE TRUST

Brussels is the capital of fries, and this cannot be said often enough. Fry shops are scattered throughout the neighbourhoods, serving as nostalgic spots where you can indulge in hand-cut potatoes, twice-fried in beef fat, sprinkled with salt and slathered in sauces with whimsical names.

Amidst the centuries-old tradition of this unconventional cuisine, a newcomer has emerged: Fernand Obb. Fernand is the name of a cat. Obb refers to Obbrussel (literally 'above Brussels'), the nickname once given to the commune of Saint-Gilles where our fry shop is located.

This place is a fresh take on the traditional fry shop. Here everything is beautiful and local. It's a haven for delicatessen items and 100% Belgian products.

FERNAND OBB DELICATESSEN
2, RUE DE TAMINES
1060 SAINT-GILLES

fernand-obb.be

Instagram: @fernand_obb

The highlight is the *gaufrite*, which captures the delightful spirit of the city: a waffle-shaped fry, cooked in rapeseed oil (because they're also vegetarian-friendly here). And let's not forget their shrimp croquettes, which contain 45% shrimp – caught off the Belgian coast, no less – and have won numerous awards. So there's no reason not to indulge!

**In Brussels, mixed heritage is a badge of honour. Yes! All Brussels locals proudly claim to be* zinneke, *which means 'mongrel' in the Brussels dialect.*

BRUSSELS
BEER PROJECT

ART NOUVEAU, BLÉROT AND A GOOD SLEEP

We're in the heart of the Ixelles Ponds district. Here, the facades compete in inventiveness and fantasy, in one of the most beautiful urban settings created in Brussels in around 1900.

Designed by architect Ernest Blérot in 1904, two of the houses stand out for their fabulous wrought ironwork with clematis motifs, which can also be seen on the floor mosaics. Identical at first glance, the facades nevertheless play on subtle differences between them.

MAISON FLAGEY
39, AVENUE DU GÉNÉRAL DE GAULLE
1050 IXELLES

+32 496 24 28 23 | maisonflagey.com | Tram and bus stop: Flagey

Oh joy! No. 39 is home to a bed and breakfast. It's just a two-minute walk from one of Brussels' party hotspots, Flagey, but also a chance to enter one of the most interesting interiors from this era, a listed monument since 1989. Here, in fact, the traditional Brussels 'three-piece-window' has been replaced by a fabulous hall that spans the entire height of the house. Each bedroom is unique, with bathrooms that you'll be telling all your friends about.

THE ELUSIVE ABBEY

La Cambre Abbey is a miracle! Since its foundation in around 1200, it has constantly escaped destruction and then urbanisation, which now surrounds it on all sides. Although unimaginable today, this Benedictine abbey, inhabited by powerful women, thrived for centuries in a virtually deserted setting on the edge of the forest.

Closed at the end of the 18th century, after a long period of neglect, since 1927 it has been home to the renowned École Nationale Supérieure des Arts Visuels, founded by Henry van de Velde in 1926 on the model of the Bauhaus. Since then, the little oasis of La Cambre has been teeming with youth and creativity.

Although enclosed, it is above all a place of peace and tranquillity, where you can enjoy a picnic or a good book – it's a wonderful time machine!

ABBAYE DE LA CAMBRE
MAIN ENTRANCE, RUE DU MONASTÈRE
1050 BRUXELLES

Open 24/7

Tram or bus stops: Abbaye, Cambre-Étoile or Étangs d'Ixelles

THE POISONOUS BEAUTY OF ART NOUVEAU

Ask anyone from Brussels and they'll tell you: art nouveau, that extraordinary pan-European artistic movement, was born in Brussels in 1893! That year, architect Victor Horta revolutionised his craft, breathing life into buildings with organic, nature-inspired forms and an unprecedented embrace of light. His vision was radical, his creations sublime.

Horta's own home has long been open to the public – you've probably visited it already (if not, go at once!). But another masterpiece, also a UNESCO World Heritage site, has more recently become accessible: the Hôtel van Eetvelde.

HÔTEL VAN EETVELDE & LAB·AN
2, AVENUE PALMERSTON
1000 BRUXELLES

lab-an.be
Instagram: @hotelvaneetvelde.brussels

Metro stop: Maelbeek

In 1895 Edmond van Eetvelde, Secretary General of the Independent State of the Congo, commissioned Horta to build a town house for his family and to host receptions as part of his duties.

Behind an almost industrial facade, the interior is breathtaking, arranged around a glass and iron winter garden. A fascinating achievement that also lifts the veil on the links between artists and the great colony of Leopold II.

WANT MORE?

INDULGE IN A DELIGHTFUL ART NOUVEAU OVERLOAD BY VISITING:

> **Hôtel Solvay**

The breathtaking 1894 masterpiece by Victor Horta, designed for the Solvay industrial family. Two options available: a guided individual tour or a self-guided visit.

224, avenue Louise - 1000 Bruxelles
hotelsolvay.be

> **Hôtel Max Hallet**

Designed by Horta in 1903, this creation is more understated, yet is still a remarkably intelligent work by the Belgian architect.

346, avenue Louise - 1000 Bruxelles
victorhorta.be

> **Maison Cauchie**

One of the most beautiful facades in Brussels. Step inside to discover an interior that reflects the artistic vision of its Belle Époque creators, Paul and Lina Cauchie.

5, rue des Francs - 1040 Etterbeek
cauchie.be

> **Maison Hannon**

Designed by architect Jules Brunfaut for the engineer Edouard Hannon and his wife Marie, this is the most French-inspired of Brussels' art nouveau houses. Pair your visit with the nearby private residence of Victor Horta.

1, avenue de la Jonction - 1060 Saint-Gilles
maisonhannon.be

NOT ALL ART **IS CAST AWAY**

Behind the impressive Art and History Museum, which comes highly recommended (it's an incredible place, a sort of Belgian version of the British Museum), lies an extraordinary and rare venue that offers a complete immersion in the masterpieces of art history: the Cinquantenaire Moulding Workshop.

Established over 130 years ago, it houses nearly 5,000 moulds of major works from some of the finest European museums. Interestingly, it is still in operation and sells reproductions of ancient artworks, from prehistory to the 18th century. Here, you can purchase a Discobolus, a Michelangelo slave, an Assyrian lion, a Voltaire or even a Manneken Pis.

As a conservatory of ancient techniques (moulding, chiselling, patina), it also offers the public the chance to wander through its storerooms every Thursday afternoon and, once a month, to take part in a unique guided tour ... What a vibe!

ATELIER DE MOULAGE DU CINQUANTENAIRE
10, PARC DU CINQUANTENAIRE
1000 BRUXELLES

Guided tours for individuals once a month, see: artandhistory.museum/fr/atelier-de-moulage

Metro stops: Schuman or Mérode

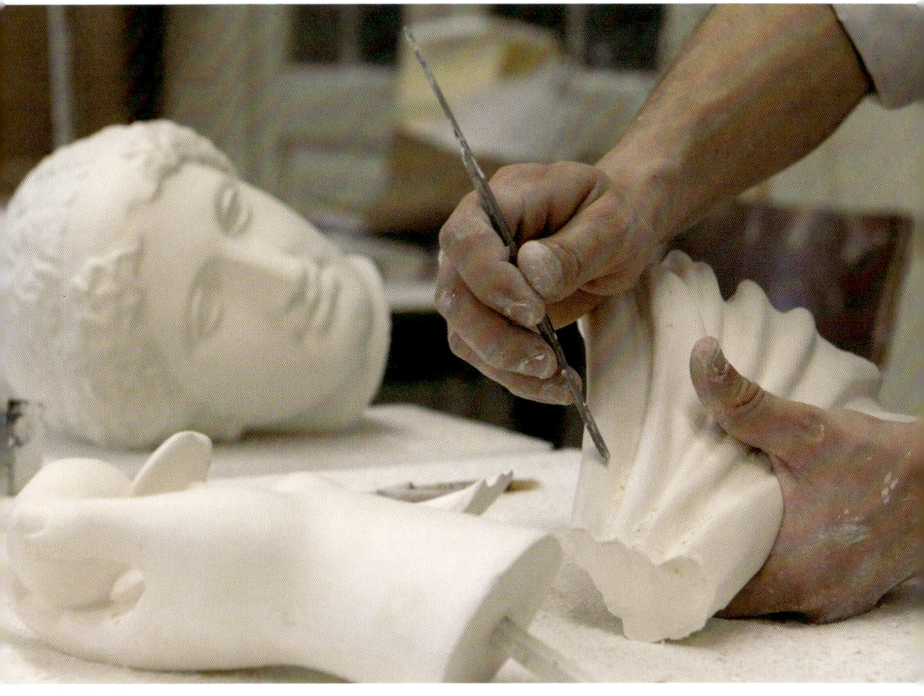

HALLUCINATE
IN A HISTORIC HOUSE

Untouched by passing trends and a little out of date, this house is frozen in time and still echoes with the presence of its former occupants.

Built in 1836 by the then-famous painter Eugène Verboeckhoven, it was occupied from 1844 by one of the most fascinating women of the Romantic era, the virtuoso Marie Pleyel. This sublime concert pianist was loved by Berlioz, Chopin, Liszt, Dumas and many others who came here. It was she who had the small music salon built at the end of the courtyard, and it was in this house that she died in 1875.

DE ULTIEME HALLUCINATIE RESTAURANT
316, RUE ROYALE
1210 SAINT-JOSSE-TEN-NOODE

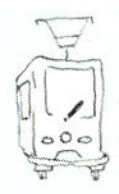

ultiemehallucinatie.be
Instagram: @de_ultieme_hallucinatie

Tram stop: Gillon or Sainte-Marie

TOONE

In 1904 the house was given a new lease of life and gained its current appearance. It was transformed in the geometric art nouveau style by a talented young architect, Paul Hamesse, for the Cohn-Donnay family. Nothing escaped the stylisation, from the umbrella stand to the billiards table, from the billiards table to the chandeliers. It's exceptional.

In the 1980s it became a bar-restaurant, De Ultieme Hallucinatie (The Ultimate Hallucination), and its garden was covered over. Legend has it that Kasparov played a game of chess here and the Belgian singer Arno worked in the kitchen. So many hallucinations to indulge in when you come for a drink!

AN URBAN PLANNING MISTAKE THAT ONLY BRUSSELS CAN CLAIM

It is well known that Brussels is one of the most multicultural cities in the world. Straddling Schaerbeek and Saint-Josse, the Turkish quarter is known as 'Little Anatolia' as it's home to a whole village from Anatolia, Emirdağ, which produces delicious elongated Turkish pizzas known as *pide*.

In the heart of this district, in a calm and surprising location, lies one of those urban planning mistakes that Brussels is known for: the Eenens-Terlinden Castle, now commonly referred to as the Maison des Arts (House of Arts).

RESTAURANT L'ESTAMINET AND LA MAISON DES ARTS
147, CHAUSSÉE DE HAECHT
1030 SCHAERBEEK

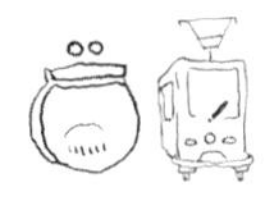

+32 2 240 34 99
lamaisondesarts.be
Instagram: @estaminet1030

Tram and bus stops: Robiano or Sainte-Marie

pour financer des actions solidaires,
comme le dîner solidaire mensuel
à l'estaminet

Built in 1826, at a time when Brussels' suburbs were still fields, this beautiful residence and a tiny part of its garden miraculously escaped urban development.

The former stables now house L'Estaminet, a charming place to enjoy delicious, locally sourced food at affordable prices, all set against a backdrop of warm oak panelling and chestnut-wood tables. When the weather is nice, you can also take advantage of the terrace and garden – an ideal setting for a quiet moment alone or a memorable gathering with friends.

Right next door, the Maison des Arts regularly hosts excellent free contemporary art exhibitions.

CLOSER **TO HEAVEN**

The ways of the Lord are, as we know, mysterious. So too is the path taken by St Anthony of Padua Church in the municipality of Forest, just a short distance from the Gare du Midi.

The history of this place of worship is a fascinating reflection of the times, stretching back centuries. When Forest was still a village, a small chapel stood here, dedicated to St Anthony, the patron saint of livestock, believed to protect animals from disease. As urbanisation took hold in the late 19th and early 20th centuries, the chapel was replaced in 1907 by a proper parish church. But as secularisation grew, the congregation dwindled and the church was slowly abandoned – until 2022, when four fanatical climbers gave it a new lease of life as an indoor climbing gym.

CLIMBING GYM MANIAK PADOUE
26, RUE DES MOINES
1190 FOREST

Guided climbs on reservation
padoue.maniak.club

Metro stop: Gare du Midi

Today, beneath the glow of a grand stained-glass window, visitors can try three different types of climbing: lead climbing (with ropes), bouldering (without ropes, over thick crash mats) and speed climbing. New to the sport? No worries – everything is in place to guide you. Booking is simple and can be done online. Easy.

THE MOST BEAUTIFUL GREENHOUSES IN THE WORLD

Built from glass and steel to match the ambitions of Belgium's extravagant King Leopold II, the Laeken Greenhouses are directly adjacent to the royal residence. This stunning grand complex includes over 20 greenhouses of varying sizes and purposes (dining room, cloakroom, landing area, church and more), covering more than 700 metres.

Taking more than 30 years to build, at the end of the 19th century, the greenhouses were designed by Alphonse Balat, Victor Horta's mentor. They embody a style that hints at the emerging art nouveau movement: a transparent architecture supported by a metal framework that elevates and celebrates the beauty of the plant world.

SERRES ROYALES DE LAEKEN
AVENUE DU PARC ROYAL
1020 LAEKEN

For opening dates and reservations: koninklijke-serres-royales.be

Bus stop: Serres royales

Inside, the greenhouses are home to botanical wonders – a miniature world tour of global flora, right in the heart of Brussels. Among the standout collections are the towering palms, 200-year-old orange trees and an exquisite array of camellias.

The greenhouses are only open to the public for a few days in the spring, a tradition decreed by Leopold II himself. It's an unmissable event. But be aware that tickets are now sold exclusively online.

PHOTOS © A. ROBYNS

ALREADY A TASTE **OF THE FOREST**

The Bois de la Cambre is one of the largest parks in Brussels, of which there are many. These 122 hectares, on the edge of the Sonian Forest, were laid out around 1865 according to the principles of English landscaping, which were in vogue at the time: irregular planting and paths, alternating clumps of trees and beautiful open spaces, picturesque scenes such as a lake with an island, a rustic bridge, and so on.

When you go to the 'BDC', as teenagers call it, you enter right into the life of Brussels. As soon as the sun comes out, the whole city comes here to picnic, lie down, run around and chat. Admittedly, it can get pretty crowded.

But at the end of the wood, there's a clearing where you can enjoy a drink in the evening or a snack during the day.

With its tall beech trees, this place is like a prelude to the nearby forest.

KIOSQUE DU BOIS DE LA CAMBRE
AVENUE DES GENÊTS
1000 BRUXELLES

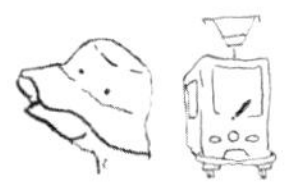

Tram stop: Legrand

DRINKS
FOOD
ESG

LE KIOSQUE
Plat du moment
POULET
MARDI
Stand-Up
MERCREDI
JAZZ
VENDREDI
Drink in the Woods
Carte des Vins
Service à table!

A CATHEDRAL
OF TREES

One of Brussels' most breathtaking features is the vast forest that borders its eastern and southern edges. The Sonian Forest, spanning nearly 5,000 hectares, is a sanctuary of towering beech trees, their slender trunks rising like the columns of a grand cathedral. This was once the hunting ground of the Dukes of Burgundy and later rulers like Charles V, who rode out in a display of grandeur that would be unthinkable today.

This forest is like the city's divine mother. It's easy to reach by public transport, and once there, you can wander for hours. In the past, it was dotted with monasteries and parts of one of them, the Rouge-Cloître Priory, are still standing. It's well worth a visit as the place radiates a sense of peace, intimately connected to the calm of the surrounding woods.

The 700-metre-long wall surrounding the priory sums up its history: it symbolises the limits that the community imposed

ROUGE-CLOÎTRE
RUE DU ROUGE-CLOÎTRE
1160 AUDERGHEM

auderghem.be/rouge-cloitre

JARDIN MASSART
1850, CHAUSSÉE DE WAVRE
1160 AUDERGHEM

info@environnement.brussels
Metro stop: Hermann-Debroux
Tram stop: Auderghem-Forêt

upon itself to remain separate from the world; it played a useful defensive role in five centuries of wars; and lastly, it confirms the self-sufficiency of the priory, which was almost like a small independent town.

On-site, a variety of activities are possible: you can enjoy a light meal, take a walk in the forest or visit the nearby Jean Massart Botanical Garden, a wonderful place managed by the University of Brussels.

THE *ENFANT TERRIBLE* OF BRUSSELS' GASTRONOMY

Fervent and passionate, he's a master of flavours, with culinary finesse. For 30 years, Christophe Hardiquest has reigned over gastronomy from Brussels. In 2001 he opened his restaurant, Bon Bon, which was awarded two Michelin stars. He himself was named Chef of the Year in 2010 by Gault&Millau, which is no small feat!

In 2023 he rolled the dice again and created an unusual gastronomic counter with 22 high chairs, partly inspired by the nearby Sonian Forest and Belgian terroir. The kitchen is open and everything is cooked before your eyes, making the experience fully immersive. It's organic, creative, human and sustainable all in one go ...

MENSSA
453, AVENUE DE TERVUEREN
1150 WOLUWE-SAINT-PIERRE

+32 2 346 66 15

menssa.be
Instagram: @christophe.hardiquest

© MARELUNE YVINEC, NOUVELLE LUNE AGENCY

© MAURICE JACCARD

© MAURICE JACCARD

In Brussels, a growing trend in recent years has been to rethink dining by embracing seasonal ingredients, natural produce and sustainable practices. Chefs create with what's available, here and now. The result? A handful of exciting restaurants led by young, innovative chefs – perfect for culinary adventurers.

ENTROPY
22, PLACE SAINT-GÉRY
1000 BRUXELLES

Chef Elliott Van de Velde elected Young Chef 2025 by the Gault&Millau guide

entropyrestaurant.be

IODA

© IODA

IODA

© IODA

SAVAGE

© SAVAGE

SAVAGE

© SAVAGE

IODA
23, RUE DE LA VICTOIRE
1060 SAINT-GILLES

ioda.be
Instagram: @ioda.restaurant

SAVAGE
22, RUE DE LA PAIX
1050 BRUXELLES

savage.restaurant
Instagram: @savage.restaurant

LISTEN TO THE BEATING HEART OF **OLD ANDERLECHT**

Brussels is a mosaic of 19 communes, each with its own distinct spirit. Anderlecht, in particular, has retained its soul. Here, there are no crowds of visitors – only the quiet delight of experiencing a place that has remained true to itself, untouched by the noisy and restless tide of modern life.

Take the metro to Saint-Guidon station. A short walk away, you'll find Place de la Vaillance, a square with a distinctly Flemish Grand-Place feel. It's dominated by the beautifully contoured silhouette of the Collegiate Church of Sts Peter and Guidon, once a renowned pilgrimage site.

Step inside. Typical of the local Gothic style, the church is more compact than its French counterparts, nurturing a sense of calm and serenity.

PLACE DE LA VAILLANCE
BETWEEN RUE PORSELEIN AND RUE DU CHAPELAIN
1170 ANDERLECHT

Metro stop: Saint-Guidon

As you leave, don't miss Rue Porselein, a charming cobbled street that has retained its medieval narrowness. Another hidden gem lies just behind the church: Belgium's smallest *béguinage*. This unique institution, both religious and secular, was reserved for women who lived in chastity and obedience – but without taking perpetual vows, meaning they could leave the community whenever they wished. Under the *ancien régime*, this was the greatest degree of freedom a woman could hope for ...

> Just beyond Place de la Vaillance stands what is known as the Erasmus House in Anderlecht, though in reality the great humanist only lived here for a short time. Today, it houses a fascinating museum that delves into Erasmus' life and the Renaissance world in which he lived.

But it's not just the museum's interiors that make this place worth a visit – the gardens are equally remarkable. Simply ask for the key at the entrance. The first garden is a neatly arranged quadrangle filled with medicinal plants, used in the past to treat headaches, kidney stones and dysentery.

Beyond it lies a philosophical garden, offering shade beneath ancient beech trees and featuring artworks. Among them, small pools designed by Marie-Jo Lafontaine reflect Erasmus' maxims in shimmering silver letters: *Festina lente* (Make haste slowly), *Ubi amici ibi opes* (Where your friends are, there is your wealth) and the sublime *Sidera addere caelo* (To add stars to the sky), encapsulating the very essence of this extraordinary garden.

© MAISON ERASME

© MAISON ERASME

© STEFAN TAVERNIER SUPERFICIES

© STEFAN TAVERNIER SUPERFICIES

MAISON D'ÉRASME
31, RUE DE FORMANOIR
1070 ANDERLECHT

erasmushouse.museum
Instagram: @erasmushouse_beguinage

A new museum is being prepared in the former béguinage as we write these pages
Visit the website for more information

> Friture René is an absolute gem. Not only does the menu showcase the best of Brussels cuisine, but the setting is equally enchanting: old wooden window frames, chequered tablecloths, yellow ceramic tiles set into pitch-pine panelling, vintage paintings and warm, welcoming staff.

FRITURE RENÉ
14, PLACE DE LA RÉSISTANCE
1070 ANDERLECHT

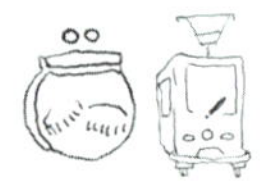

Instagram: @friturerene

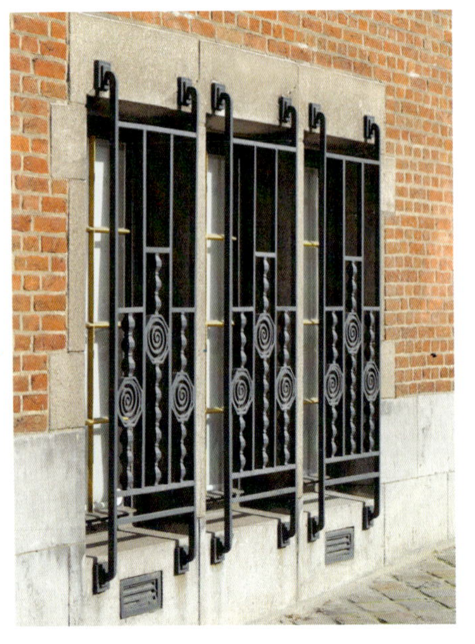

6

AND WHAT IF THE MASTERPIECE WAS THE CITY ITSELF?

Brussels is clearly a city of individual houses, each distinguished by its unique facade. These facades showcase the skills of the craftsmen who built them, the architects who contributed their designs and the ordinary people who desired and cherished them. This may seem like small-scale architecture, but when considered on the scale of the city, it becomes significant. It's a stylistic exercise, endlessly repeated across the narrow, tall surfaces of Brussels' facades.

AVENUE LOUIS BERTRAND 1030 SCHAERBEEK	ÉTANGS D'IXELLES 1050 IXELLES	HÔTEL DE VILLE DE SAINT-GILLES 1060 SAINT-GILLES
Tram stop: Saint-Servais	Bus and tram stops: Flagey	Tram stops: Barrière or Lombardie

While many cities like Paris align their cornices at the same height or follow a consistent design from one house to the next, Brussels has long embraced a delightful and charming rivalry of fierce individualism that can be seen in its streets.

The people of Brussels have had a long-standing attachment to their homes (just a glance at the Grand-Place is enough to convince you), but it was particularly from 1880, during a period of rapid urbanisation, that private architecture flourished with a boundless originality, reaching its apogee at the turn of the 19th and 20th centuries with art nouveau.

One of the great pleasures of the city is embarking on a photographic safari, searching for those stunning architectural details. There are remarkable finds everywhere but be sure not to miss Avenue Louis Bertrand in Schaerbeek, the area around the town hall in Saint-Gilles and the edges of the Ixelles Ponds. Enjoy your walk!

101
99

We never reveal the 31st address in the 'Soul of' series because it's strictly confidential. Up to you to find it!

PLEASE **DON'T TELL!**

A tall, narrow Brussels house, full of stairs. The atmosphere is chic and intimate, with refined and elegant cocktails. On the first floor, there's a well-lit bar and a smoking room adorned with delightful paintings. The depths of the house are reserved for a dance floor featuring eclectic electronic music. Two levels, two vibes, perfect for a night out!

The experience is secretive and exclusive, created by actor Jérémie Renier. You'll need to discover the password to get in. Hint: Instagram will help you ...

SECRET ADDRESS

Find the password on instagram: @jalousybrussels

ACKNOWLEDGEMENTS

THANK YOU to Bam Seck, Nico, Charlottine, Giuliano, Alex de Beauté and Alex de Suède, Axeleke, Marcel, Les Ondines, Anton, Marie-Garance, Camille-Fleur and Yvan, Petit Page, Gigi, Crochet and Huitloup, Nonote and Vivi, Céline, Ornella, Sophie Soleil, Ann, Filou, Alain and Nawal, Quentin Chaton, Guillaume, Timon and Princesse Cancan, Ben, Pol, Spiff, Elena Petit Chat, Odilon Moon and the Little Mermaid. Thank you to the enchantresses, the owners and managers of the site and the photographers.

Special thanks to Thomas, Morgane and Mado.

It was a lovely adventure.

WHAT'S NEXT?
WE DIGEST.

This book was created by:

Isabelle Douillet-de Pange, texts

Allilalu, illustrations

Emmanuelle Willard Toulemonde, layout

Olivia Fuller, translation

Jana Gough, editing

Sonny Alexander, proofreading

Thomas Jonglez, Morgane De Wulf and Mado La Quintinie, publishing

Cover photo: © Isabelle Douillet-de Pange,
Rue de la Cigogne, 1000 Bruxelles

You can write to us at info@editionsjonglez.com
Follow us on Instagram: @editionsjonglez

THANK YOU

Isabelle Douillet-de Pange was born and lives in Brussels. She is an art historian (UCL) with a passion for architecture. She worked for a long time on the inventory of architectural heritage for the Brussels-Capital Region before becoming a curator at the Museums of the City of Brussels, then at the Fondation Folon. She is the author of numerous publications about her city.

Allison Michel works as an illustrator under the name **Allilalu**. She writes and draws whenever life's fast pace gives her a moment to breathe. In 2021, she took the stage at the Live Magazine for illustrators at Bozar to present her work. In 2023, she published her first book, Mamies Blues, with Editions de la Renaissance du Livre. She has exhibited in Paris and Brussels. In her free time, she practices cup-and-ball juggling. She collects yellow objects, elderly ladies, and flat stones. You can explore her world on her blog: allilalu.com

From the same publisher

Photo Books

Abandoned America: The age of Consequences
Abandoned Asylums
Abandoned Australia
Abandoned Belgium
Abandoned Churches: Unclaimed Places of Workship
Abandoned Cinemas of the World
Abandoned France
Abandoned Germany
Abandoned Lebanon
Abandoned Italy
Abandoned Japan
Abandoned Spain
Abandoned USSR
Abandoned World - An AI-generated exploration
After the Final Curtain: The Fall of the American Movie Theater
After the Final Curtain: America's Abandoned Theaters
Baikonur - Vestiges of the Soviet Space Program
Cinemas - A French Heritage
Chernobyl's Atomic Legacy - 25 years after disaster
Clickbait - A visual journey through AI-generated stories
Destination: Wellness - Our 35 best places in the world to make a pause
Forbidden Places - Exploring our Abandoned Heritage
Forbidden France
Forgotten Heritage
Private Islands for Rent
Oblivion
Secret Sacred Sites
Unusual Hotels Europe
Unusual Hotels - World
Unusual Hotels UK & Ireland
Unusual Nights in Paris
Unusual Shopping in Paris
Unusual Wines
Venice deserted

'Soul of' Guides

Soul of Amsterdam - A guide to the 30 best experiences
Soul of Athens - A guide to 30 exceptional experiences
Soul of Barcelona - 30 experiences
Soul of Berlin - A guide to the 30 best experiences
Soul of Detroit - A guide to exceptional experiences
Soul of Kyoto - A guide to 30 exceptional experiences
Soul of Lisbon - A guide to exceptional experiences
Soul of Los Angeles - A guide to 30 exceptional experiences
Soul of Marrakesh - A guide to 30 exceptional experiences
Soul of Marseille - A guide to exceptional experiences
Soul of Milan - A guide to exceptional experiences
Soul of New York - A guide to 30 exceptional experiences
Soul of Paris - 30 experiences
Soul of Rome - A guide to exceptional experiences
Soul of Tokyo - A guide to exceptional experiences
Soul of Venice - A guide to 30 exceptional experiences
Soul of Vienna - A guide to exceptional experiences

Atlas

Atlas of forbidden places
Atlas of geographical curiosities
Atlas of extreme weather
Atlas of unusual wines

'Secret' Guides

Secret Amsterdam
Secret Bali - An unusual guide
Secret Bangkok
Secret Barcelona
Secret Bars & Restaurants in Paris
Secret Bath - An unusual guide
Secret Belfast
Secret Berlin
Secret Boston - An unusual guide
Secret Brighton - An unusual guide
Secret Brooklyn
Secret Brussels
Secret Budapest
Secret Buenos Aires
Secret Campania
Secret Cape Town
Secret Copenhagen
Secret Corsica
Secret Dolomites
Secret Dublin - An unusual guide
Secret Edinburgh - An unusual guide
Secret Florence
Secret French Riviera
Secret Geneva
Secret Glasgow
Secret Granada
Secret Helsinki
Secret Istanbul
Secret Johannesburg
Secret Lisbon
Secret Liverpool - An unusual guide
Secret London - An unusual guide
Secret London - Unusual Bars & Restaurants
Secret Los Angeles - An unusual guide
Secret Louisiana
Secret Madrid
Secret Mexico City
Secret Milan
Secret Montreal - An unusual guide
Secret Naples
Secret New Orleans - An unusual guide
Secret New York - An unusual guide
Secret New York - Curious Activities
Secret New York - Hidden Bars & Restaurants
Secret Normandy
Secret Paris
Secret Postdam
Secret Prague
Secret Provence
Secret Rio
Secret Rome
Secret Seville
Secret Singapore
Secret Stockholm
Secret Sussex - An unusual guide
Secret Tokyo
Secret Tuscany
Secret Venice
Secret Vienna
Secret Washington DC - An unusual guide

Follow us on Facebook and Instagram

Registration of copyright: May 2025 - Edition: 01
ISBN: 978-2-36195-819-0
Printed in Slovakia by Polygraf